Adult
Handbook

Lessons of a Father for His
Favorite Son

CRAIG SYLVES

ISBN 978-1-68570-576-3 (paperback)
ISBN 978-1-68570-577-0 (digital)

Christian Faith Publishing
832 Park Avenue
Meadville, PA 16335
www.christianfaithpublishing.com

Printed in the United States of America

For
DUNCAN ERIK SYLVES
My favorite son

From
CRAIG R. SYLVES
His favorite father

August 3, 2002

Top Ten Rules

Introduction

This book started as a joke. One day, when Duncan was about eight years old, his mother and I took him out on a Friday night to look at furniture. It was a hot summer night, and I had not changed out of my dress work clothes. We decided to stop at a hamburger drive-in restaurant, and since it was hot, we ate outside at their picnic tables. Duncan asked me why I had long pants on instead of shorts, and I told him that I had to wear long pants on a Friday night. He asked why, and for some reason, I said because it was required. He said where did I get that information, and I said, "It is in the adult handbook."

"What is the handbook?" he asked.

I told him that he would get this when he turns eighteen. Duncan always has a good sense of humor, and he and I always teased each other since he was a very small child. For many years after that, every time he asked me one of his millions of *why* questions, I often told him it was in the "handbook." This became such a family joke that my mother-in-law told me that I should write this book just to be fair to Duncan, so I did.

Duncan, I have told you all your life that you were my favorite son. Yes, you are my only son (child, to be exact), but I truly mean that you are my favorite. I once told you that if God came to me and gave me the option of choosing any son in the world, I would choose you—and that still applies. You were the best birthday gift anyone could ever have received. I wanted to write this book to pass on some of the things I have learned in my life, and hopefully if others read this book, it will be of benefit to them too. Son, I am very proud of you, and I know you have greatness inside of you. But it is up to you to attain this greatness. We all have the spark of God in us. We all have the opportunity and free will to become the best we can, and we also have the free will to waste our lives. I hope you choose a path that will leave the earth a better place after your time is done here.

What will the world say about Duncan E. Sylves? Are you honest? Are you trustworthy? Is your word your bond? Are you a good friend and partner? You will make mistakes in life as we all do but the key is to determine *now* who you are and never deviate from you. If you decide now who, you are, many decisions later in life will be easier to make. Do what is right regardless if it is easier or harder to do. Remember, never do anything in the dark that you would be embarrassed about in the light.

I never knew how hard my parents worked for us kids until I became a father. When the time comes for you to be a father, I hope you will remember all the things we did together and all the things I did for you. I want only one thing in return, and that is for you to be the best dad you can be for your children. That would be the greatest gift you could give to me.

I hope this book will give you a good start in your new life as an adult. Always be true to yourself, and remember that your father loves you and that I am here for you. I have faith in you and I know you will be a successful person; and if you take to heart what I have written, you can be ten times the man I am. Go in peace and go with God.

Your loving father

Feed Your Body

The Essence of Survival

> Every morning in Africa, a gazelle wakes up.
> It knows it must run faster than the fastest lion or
> it will be killed…every morning a lion wakes up.
> It knows it must outrun the slowest gazelle or it
> will starve to death. It doesn't matter whether you
> are a lion or a gazelle… When the sun comes up,
> you had better be running.

> Spirit is the life, mind is the builder, physical is the result. (Edgar Cayce)

Your body is your temple. This is where we meet our God. Your body is your vehicle—your transportation to the physical places your spirit wants to go. Take care of your body so you can get to the places you want and need to go to, and also, so you can have the longest life possible, allowing you the chance to accomplish your mission here.

In computer terms, "garbage in, garbage out" means the quality of results you get out of the computer correlates directly to the quality of the information you put in. This applies to your own body. You put junk in, you get junk out. I have never understood why most people take better care of their cars than themselves. I was never very athletic until about three years after college when I took up running. I ended up running about twenty-five races a year. Some were five miles, ten miles, half marathons (13.1 miles), and a few marathons

(26.2 miles). I ran almost every day for about fifteen years. At age thirty, I took up karate, taught, and worked out for almost twenty years. At age fifty, I still run, although not so many miles, and I can still fight and keep up with most eighteen-year-olds in class. The only reason I mention this is that physical exercise will keep you young, give you the positive brain chemicals (endorphins), and help ward off illnesses. When you exercise, your body works better, you feel better, you eat better, and unless you get run over by a bus, you will live longer. Everything about exercise is positive as long as you keep it within reason.

The great thing about exercise is the body will tell you what you need if you listen. Proper nutrition will not only help you function properly, but it will also help you think better, handle stress better, live longer (perhaps), and most importantly, live better. It doesn't matter if it is running, biking, soccer, treadmill, or rowing. Aerobic exercise is much more important than anaerobic exercise. Aerobic involves air, so anything that brings in more air is better for your body in the long run than anaerobic exercise, such as lifting weights. Lifting weights is fine too, but don't do that exclusively without any aerobic exercise.

One of the most important areas of health I discovered is proper vitamin and mineral supplements and making the body alkaline. There is a ton of readily available information on vitamins so you can do your own research, but I believe the concept of alkalinity is probably one of the most important areas of concern. Foods and emotions change the acid/alkaline balance of the body. Viruses such as the cold virus thrive in an acid environment. Lack of the proper eight hours of sleep, stress, and the wrong diet all change the body from alkaline to acidic. Observe children that eat a lot of sugar, and you will see kids with a lot of colds and other illnesses. Observe children that eat very little sugar, eat properly, and exercise, and you will see these children aren't sick very often, behave better, and often get better grades. Poor diet can have a huge impact on the success you have, and I think more importantly, on your self-esteem.

If you can't think, you can't perform well, and you begin to think you are not very smart or very good at what you do. A simple change in diet can have a huge effect on who you are. If you feel good, feel alert, feel energetic, you will be able to accomplish much more in life, you will feel better about yourself, and you will have a much more positive impact on this world. Life looks very different when you feel good than when you don't.

With all your soccer playing in the past, you know how important exercise and nutrition is. Because college will require a lot of your time for study, college students who aren't part of a formal athletic program often start to gain weight and pick up bad eating habits. Exercise and diet are two parts of an effective health program that will impact your college life—physically, mentally, and spiritually. You know what to do.

Feed Your Mind

The Power of Attitude

> Our lives are not determined by what happens to us, but how we react to what happens, not by what life brings to us, but by the attitude we bring to life. A positive attitude causes a chain reaction of positive thoughts, events and outcomes. It is a catalyst, a spark that creates extraordinary results.

> Wisdom is knowing what path to take next. Integrity is taking it!

Knowledge is what you absorb from books and people. Wisdom is taking that knowledge and being able to use it in a positive, productive manner. Both are important, but wisdom is what will set you apart from the rest. It will give you the edge you need to succeed. As an older adult, I can tell you many adults have knowledge, but very few have wisdom. Be careful of who you listen to because if you listen to those who simply have knowledge and no wisdom, you will be led down the wrong path. Listen to that little small voice that resides inside of you for the true wisdom.

So how do you feed your mind? Read, talk to older people, search out the truth. Turn off the TV, turn off the music, turn off the computer and computer games, and take time to read books that will enrich your life. Read history so you don't have to repeat the mistakes of others. Read science to keep up with the ever-changing growth

13

of knowledge. Read the Bible, books about people of the Bible, and Bible history. Read magazines, newspapers, and politics since you have to live in this world. And read about the profession of your choice so you can stay current and do the best job you can.

I used to get laughed at by my friends because of the books I was constantly reading. I can remember getting a bunch of you-know-what because I was reading a book about wood. This book described how they used to build barns and houses without any nails. It described how different wood was used, the peculiarities of that wood, and how it all fit together. I found it fascinating; my friends found it weird. I read it anyway and just laughed with them. I still have that book, and I still am glad I read it. This is my life, not theirs. I will read what I find interesting, and I really don't care what they think. You shouldn't either.

Talking to older people was one of the things I decided early in life to do. I was blessed with very loving and caring parents, grandparents, and other relatives. I always made a habit of asking them about their lives and what it was like for them growing up in a very different age. Remember that my grandparents were born in the late 1890s. They went from the Model A auto to the landing a man on the moon. TV didn't exist when my grandparents were young. What a wealth of knowledge they were. My own parents were born in the 1920, lived through the Depression, and World War II. Again, what a wonderful way to get "living history" right in your own home. I grew up in a totally different world than they did, and of course, you grew up in a very different world than me. Many of the lessons my parents learned don't apply to me, and the same goes for you and me, but there are still life lessons to learn from every generation. Seek them out, and you will be the wiser.

Dad always told me to be a lion and not a lamb. Be a leader, not a follower. It is ironic you, me, and Dad are Leos. We are lions. Lead, don't follow. You don't have to lead the crowd, but you have to lead yourself. Follow your path, not others. Having knowledge and wisdom will allow you to be able to choose this path. If all you know is digging ditches, you will be bound to a job of ditch digging. Getting your college degree is a great start, but let this be a beginning for you.

College will expose you to so much more of the world, and soon you will begin to see how much is out there.

When I was in college and had to take a religion course, I chose a course on the New Testament. I was so fascinated that the professor at the end of the course asked if I wanted to go to Israel for the summer and join him on an archaeological dig. I couldn't afford it as I would have had to pay for the trip and all my living expenses. I needed the summer to work to pay the next semester, or I would have gone. What a great opportunity that would have been, but needless to say, I have been fascinated with biblical archaeology ever since. You just never know what doors will open once you begin your quest for knowledge.

Finally, search out the truth. Truth is everywhere. Truth is in the Bible and other religious books. The truth is found by listening to others and by using your inner being to sort out what is the real truth, and not just someone else's guess as to the truth. Open your eyes, open your heart, think, and mostly pray. Jesus said, "Ask and it will be given, knock and the door will be opened." As a Sunday school teacher for fourteen years, I was asked many times by students about what is proper to ask for in prayer. My answer was to ask God for wisdom first. God already knows what you need, so you should ask God for wisdom so you can do what is right. If you ask God to help you find the truth, you will be led to it. Just be sure you take time to listen as often the answer comes quietly, and if you are too busy to take time to listen, you will miss the answer.

I am excited about learning, about knowing, and about becoming the wisest person I can be. You may not know or understand what I know, what I read, or what my quest is. You may have some clues about me because of the large library of books I have, but unless you actually talk to me, you will never know. Take time to talk to others about the important things in their lives, and you will be surprised at what other people know and what they are interested in. You can learn much faster and can get to where you want to be much quicker if you take a little time and ask. You can either take a lifetime to learn something, or you can learn from others and shorten that journey, and perhaps go on to learn more new things. If you want to be smart, hang around smart people; if you want to be successful, hang around successful people. Be wise and learn from others, but be sure to pursue your quest, not theirs.

Remember the saying, "you are what you eat." The same goes for your head. You will be the same person one year from now except for the books you read, the programs or movies you watch on TV, the music you listen to, and the people you meet. Be careful of what you think about and what you dwell on as you will become that. I whispered in your ear every night that "your daddy loves you and you are a very smart young man and a very good boy." Did it work? I think your college boards prove how smart you are, so perhaps it did. I fed your head every night with positive thoughts and thoughts of how smart you were (and are). You are a little too big for me to whisper in your ear now, so it is up to you to take up where I left off. I believe feeding your head does work, so feed your head with positive thoughts, feed your head with winning thoughts, and feed your head with the thoughts of where you want to go in this life, and I know you will be able to do anything you set out to do. Remember, if you want to soar, you have to hang around with eagles, not turkeys.

Feed Your Soul

The Power of Belief

Believe in yourself. You gain strength, courage, and confidence by every experience in which you stop to look fear in the face. You must do that which you think you cannot do. (Eleanor Roosevelt)

The Light of Integrity

The soul is dyed the color of its thoughts. Think only on those things that are in line with your principles and can bear the full light of day. The content of your character is your choice. Day by day, what you choose, what you think, and what you do is who you become. Your integrity is your destiny. It is the light that guides your way. (Heraclitus)

Feeding your body is important since it is the only vehicle you have in this earthly plane. Feeding your mind will help you with your stay here, and if you attain wisdom, it will help you with the next life. Feeding your soul is what it is all about. You can do all the other things I recommend to you, but if you don't gain in your soul's growth during your stay here on earth, you have failed. Having cars, houses, toys, is not it. Yes, they make life easier, but don't ever forget: whatever you gather here on this earth stays here. Whatever you gain for your soul goes with you for eternity, and eternity is a lot longer than eighty years.

One of my favorite Bible verses is found in Matthew 6:19–21:

> Do not lay up for yourselves treasures upon earth, where moth and rust destroys, and where thieves break in and steal. But lay up for yourselves treasures in heaven, where neither moth nor rust destroys, and where thieves do not break in or steal; for where your treasure is, there will your heart be also.

We only get to rent the "stuff" we accumulate here for a little while, but the treasures of the soul are for eternity.

When you think about someone, do you think, *well, there goes John, nice car, makes lots of money, has a big house…*or do you think, *there goes John, nice guy, great friend, funny guy?* It is the latter if you really think about it. Take some time and go through your list of friends and relatives, and assign words to describe them. Money and things aren't the first things that come to mind. This is the real you. The stuff you have only tells about you—it isn't you.

You can't control others; you can only control yourself. How do you respond to people that do bad things to you? Do what I have always told you to do. Do what is right regardless of what others do to you. If someone steals from you, you have a right to protect your things and have a right to try to prevent others from taking your things; but when it happens, don't steal back, or you are just as guilty as they are. We all have to face our maker when we die to explain our actions, and yes, our thoughts. Let them explain it to their God. You may lose stuff here, you may not get the things you should get because of another, but stay the course, let them have this on their soul, you do the right thing, and you will be rewarded in the long run.

So how do you actually feed the soul? First, read the Bible. It is filled with three thousand years of stories of the relationships others had with God, and the consequences of their good and sometimes bad actions. It is a great source of information. Second, read about other people who have spent a lifetime in giving. Learn what they did, why they did it, and the results of their life. Third, spend time in meditation or just quiet listening time each day. Take time to think of the events of the day. Analyze where you are and where you are going. Ask yourself if you are proud of where you are and who you are. If no, then get about changing your life and direction. Our American life is filled with noise. TV, radio, cars, people... There is constant input and we need to turn off the world for a while, close down our external ears, and open up our internal ears to hear what our maker want us to do. Ten or fifteen minutes a day is all you need.

A guiding principle I use when I am confronted with a situation is to ask myself, *how would I explain my response to God? How would this sound when I am on the witness stand defending my life?* Don't forget, your thoughts are real too; so not only do you need to respond properly, but you also need to think properly. This applies to all aspects of your life. Your dealings with friends, enemies, loves, fellow employees, and so on. Is this decision I am about to make going to have a long term consequence, and will I like the outcome? It only takes one second to ask. If you aren't sure of the outcome, or if you don't like the outcome, don't do it. Think through the situation, visualize the potential results, and it will be easy for you to make the right decision. Ask this question on a regular basis, and you will advance your soul much more rapidly; you will save yourself from so many problems than if you just react without thinking.

Don't worry about where you need to start—just start. Read, study, question, seek. Jesus says in Matthew 7:7, "Ask, and it shall be given to you; seek and you shall find; knock, and it shall be opened to you." Ask for knowledge, ask for wisdom, ask for the right things to do, and then listen. When you ask, the answers will begin to appear. A friend may suggest a great book for you to read, you may hear a great sermon in church that pertains to a problem you have, you may take a class in school that hits the spot, or you may accidentally come across program on TV. It may also come in a dream, or it may be that still small voice within you. It is a little spooky sometimes when these things happen, but it won't happen if you don't ask. Stay tuned into the Big Guy and the answers will come.

Prayer is different from meditation. Meditation is non-active listening. It is listening to the silence. Prayer is active talking and listening. Pray for guidance and not for things. Don't pray to God to have him help you pass a test you did not study for. Ask him for help, so you can keep all the new experiences you will be having in their proper perspective and stay on track. When it comes to things, I always just say to God, "If you want me to have this, it will be. If not, then you have a reason for it and I will accept it." God already knows what you need. Notice I said need and not want. If you are in tune with God, all of your needs will be met. Not all of your wants may be met, and you will just have to understand there is a reason. Move on.

Finally, don't "practice" your religion, live your religion. As a Christian, just live by the rules. (They are in the Bible, by the way.) Make up your mind that you aren't going to kill, steal, covet (that means to want what someone else has to the point of jealousy), don't lie about others, don't commit adultery, judge others the way you want to be judged, love God with all your heart, all your mind, and all your soul, and love your neighbor as yourself. If you decide these things up-front, when the temptations come—and they will—you already know the answer. Remember, if you don't stand for something, you will fall for anything. By making up your mind now, your life will be infinitely easier later. Make these rules part of your life. Just do them; you don't need to explain them to anybody. When people give me grief about a decision I make that I know to be right, I simply tell them, "They can live by whatever rules they want to, and I will live by mine." Conversation is over; thanks for your interest. They will either think you are a total nit, or they will respect you for your commitments. Either way, it doesn't matter to me. I have to account for me, and that is exactly what I will do. Do the same, and you will have a great life.

One last note on this area. Edgar Cayce once said that "we are constantly meeting ourselves." Every so often, stand back and look at the group of people you are with. Do you like who they are? Are you like them? Every day is an opportunity to be someone new. This is your life. Put out what you want back. Remember, we reap what we sow. Sow good, you get back good. Sow junk, you get junk back. It's your choice.

Set Goals

The Essence of Achievement

> The credit belongs to those people who are actually in the arena...who know the great enthusiasms, the great devotion to a worthy cause; who at best, know the triumph of high achievement; and who, at worst, fail while daring greatly...so that their place shall never be with those cold and timid souls who know neither victory nor defeat. (Theodore Roosevelt)

Daring Adventures

> The most daring of all endeavors...to meet the shadowy future without fear and conquer the unknown. (Ferdinand Magellan, 1520)

Goals give you power and energy. Think about how much you can get done when you are trying to get ready to go out and have fun. You can clean your room, shower, iron, eat, and get out the door in thirty minutes. Now think about how long it took you to clean or attempt to clean your room when you had all Saturday afternoon to do so. It just never got done, and you wasted the entire afternoon doing so. Why the difference? Goals. You got everything done in thirty minutes because you were motivated by something greater than the stuff you had to do.

Goals also give you direction, so your energies are pooled and focused in one direction. When you have three or four things to do at the same time, you feel like your foot is nailed to the floor. You just seem to go round and round. You are distracted, and nothing seems to get done. When you have a goal, you can focus all your mental, physical, and spiritual energies in one direction, and all the distractions seem to be pushed aside. You can be the world's greatest marksman, but if you have a blindfold on, you can't hit a thing. Focus takes off the blindfold and allows you to see the target.

Goals also let you know when to stop. Now that may sound a bit funny, but as you get older, you will see people in a constant state of confusion. Having goals and hitting them, you know when you have succeeded, and you will know when to stop and move on to another goal. Zig Zigler says that "in order for you to be the winner you were born to be, you have to plan to win, you have to prepare to win, and then and only then can you legitimately expect to win. You have to *be* before you can *do* and you have to *do* before you can *have*." Plan your goals and then go out and get them.

So how do you set goals? There are three ranges of goals you should set. Short-term (up to one year), midrange (one to five years), and long-range (over five years). Long-range goals can be that you want to retire to a house overlooking the Mediterranean Sea, or as generic as having $4,000 a month in retirement income. These goals set the stage for your shorter-term goals. Midrange goals might be to graduate from college with a 4.0 grade point average. They might also be that you want to have a job working for Walt Disney after you graduate. These goals require you to make some decisions and to stick to them, or you will not be able to accomplish the goal. These goals are the ones that drive you every day. These give you the energy to study every day, to work hard, to constantly figure out what you need to do next to reach them. Short-term goals can be daily ones like make class on time; monthly, such as making the cut on the college soccer team; or a couple of months, such as make $2,000 over the summer so you can buy books and have some spending money. These, too, require you to constantly think of the goal and to use that as your motivation. These may require you to break down the steps to reach the goal. Example: if you need $2,000 and you only have fifteen weeks to work at forty hours a week, then you need to find a job paying $9.00 an hour to accomplish this goal. Short-term goals may change often as they may be reached quickly.

A technique I used when I started my insurance agency, with no money coming in, was to go out, get a photo of the Mercedes Benz I wanted, and tape it to the wall right in front of my desk, so I could see it at all times. Many days I was discouraged because of the lack of money that was coming in, but when I looked at the car of my dreams, I got energy, stopped the woe is me stuff, and got back on the phone. In two years' time, I had my car. Sweet victory!

Goals and goal setting really works. Sit down and make three lists. Short, mid, and long range. Put down some goals that you know you can hit, put down some goals that will require some extra effort, and put down some really tough ones. Having some that you will reach will give you a good feeling. It is like a pat on the back, and it will give you the desire and courage to go after the slightly harder ones, and then on to the really tough ones. Think of them as a to-do list. I make a to-do list every day. I like finding my lists and seeing that I did everything. I know that I did what I needed to do, and I know if I make another list, I can do them too. Again, it gives strength and energy.

Finally, the short-term goals will pop up and go off the list quickly. The mid-and-long-term ones will have to be looked at every so often to be sure you are on the right track, and to be sure these are still the right goals. Financial freedom at retirement will require to you set up a plan and stick with it for decades, but as you well know, investments can change over time, and they will have to be looked at from time to time. You may decide the house overlooking the Mediterranean has changed to a nice two-story house in Maine with a special addition for your favorite father. It is okay to change these goals as long as the financial plan is still in place.

As I mentioned earlier, your goals are just that—yours. Listen to others for advice on how to get there, but don't let anybody steal your dreams. I have done the things I wanted to do regardless of what friends or family have said. I listened to what they said, thanked them for their input, and then lived *my* life *my* way.

Two last items on goals. First, never give up. Only the people who quit lose. You will have many setbacks. I have had a ton. I still know what I want, and I am still working for that. I don't quit, and I hope you won't either. Secondly, as far as financial goals are concerned, always pay yourself first. In other words, start immediately to set aside money on a regular basis. Have the money come right out of your paycheck. You won't miss it. Your spending will adjust to meet your income. You will have many choices to make in life. Ask yourself each time if the specific item you want to spend money on will help you to get to your goals or not. If not, then don't do it. These are the choices all of us make. The problem with choosing now over later is when you get to later, there is no way to make up for the lost time. Something like 95 percent of all people are either dead or dead broke when they reach sixty-five. Do yourself a favor: start now and stick to it regardless.

Be of Service to Others

Benediction: Highland Presbyterian Church

Go out into the world in peace; have courage, hold on to what is good; return no man evil for evil; strengthen the fainthearted, support the weak, help the suffering; honor all men for what they could be in Christ; love and serve the Lord, rejoicing in the power of the Holy Spirit. The grace of the Lord Jesus Christ and the love of God and the fellowship of the Holy Spirit be with you.

Prayer of St. Francis of Assissi

Lord, make me an instrument of thy peace;
Where there is hatred, let me sow love;
Where there is injury, pardon;
Where there is doubt, faith;
Where there is despair, hope;
Where there is darkness, light; and
Where there is sadness, joy.

Divine Master,
Grant that I may not so much seek to be
Consoled as to console;
To be understood as to understand;
To be loved as to love;

For it is in giving that we receive;
It is in pardoning that we are pardoned;
And it is in dying that we are born
To eternal life.

" There is no greater gift a man can give than to lay down his life for another." Jesus said this two thousand years ago. This is the ultimate sacrifice one person can give to another. Would you be willing to give your life for one of your friends or family? As your father, I would willingly give my life for yours—no questions, no hesitations. I made that decision many years ago when you were born. My choice, my decision. I felt if I had the responsibility of providing for your care until you became an adult, I should be willing to give 100 percent. You need to think about how far you would go for your friends and family. This is a huge decision. You don't have to answer this right away as it is the ultimate decision anyone can make, but you should begin to think about these things. There may be a time you have to decide how far you will go for someone else. Life is precious and should not be thrown away capriciously, so start thinking about this so you can be ready if the time arrives.

I cut out a saying from the newspaper way back when I was in college that said, "Live your life so even the undertaker is sorry when you are gone." I taped that to the wall in my bedroom and looked at that every day. It is important to leave this world a better place than it was before you got here. Making money and gathering things are only good if you use them for the betterment of this world. Too many people in the business community spend their life trying to get things for themselves. This is not bad in itself, but if they step on others, make others pay for their greed, and then never do anything good with what they get, what have they gained? Remember, whatever "stuff" we get here, we have to leave when we are gone. If you don't use your gain for good, it is not good for your soul's growth. In fact, a life of greed can retard your soul's growth and cause a delay in your progress back to our maker.

The list of what you can do with your life is endless. You can be like Mother Teresa of India and dedicate your life to the poor, or you can be like Bill Gates and become the richest man in the world. I don't know what Bill does with his money, but for his soul's sake, I hope he is giving a goodly portion to good causes. You can do something to help the elderly, you can help out at a charity, you can teach Sunday school—whatever it is you feel pulled toward, just do it. Let your heart tell you what you need to do.

I want to tell you a few things I have done because many of these happened before you arrived here, and perhaps you don't know. I was on the board of the Lancaster Cancer Society for three years. I was the senior citizen insurance advisor at the Community Hospital for three years. (This was a free service I provided to any senior citizen that had a question on insurance.) I am an ordained deacon in the Presbyterian Church and went once a month up to the Schock Presbyterian Home in Mount Joy for three years and provided entertainment for the residents. I taught Sunday school for fourteen years. I taught karate for twenty years, I was in the Optimist Club that provided a yearly wrestling tournament for young wrestlers, and also had a yearly Christmas party for the local retarded citizens group. This is only a small listing of the things I have done over the course of my life. I don't tell you these things to make me look good, but I tell you these things so you can get an idea of the ways you can serve your fellow man.

Give out of love and never give thinking that you will receive some reward. The reward is knowing that you did good.

Work Hard

The Essence of Success

Successful is the person who has lived well, laughed often and loved much, who has gained the respect of children, who leaves the world better than they found it, who has never lacked appreciation for the earth beauty, who never fails to look for the best in others or give the best of themselves.

The Courage to Succeed

The sea is dangerous and its storms terrible, but these obstacles have never been sufficient reason to remain ashore...unlike the mediocre, intrepid spirits seek victory over these things that seem impossible...it is with an iron will that they embark on the most daring of all endeavors....to meet the shadowy future without fear and conquer the unknown. (Ferdinand Magellan, 1520)

As you go from childhood where everything is given to you, to adulthood where you will find that nothing is given to you, the sooner you learn this new reality—the sooner you can take your place in the universe. Everything of value will require you to go "out and get it." Nothing comes easy. If you want to be successful, you need to understand this. Study the successful people of the world and you will see they are hard workers, often putting in more study time, more desk time, more time thinking and planning than the average person. Even the very wealthy often work harder than people that have very little and could really use more. Those that have made it know that if they want to keep what they have and perhaps have more, they must never stop working. I have often heard people say that if they could make (fill in the blank), they would have it made. What they don't realize is that their spending rises to meet their income, and when they get there, often they are not really any better off, and they can't stop working as they thought they could. The more toys you have, the more you have to work to keep them. Life is littered with the bodies of those who sat back after they got to a place they thought they could sit back and rest.

Be happy about what you have, but don't be content with what you have. Always strive to do better. If you are happy with what you have, you will enjoy the journey of getting to where you want to be. If you are constantly unhappy with what you have, the journey will not be pleasant, and you will waste so much of your life. Enjoy the journey, enjoy the struggle, enjoy the mistakes you will make, learn from the mistakes, and keep on moving. Moving is the key.

Find a job you love to do, and you will find it is infinitely more enjoyable, and you will find how easy it is to work hard at it. In fact, it may not even feel like work. Have a job that you don't like, and you will find that you have no energy to do this job, and everything will seem like such a heavy load.

When you work, leave the problems of home at home; and when you get home, leave the problems of the office there. Most people take their personal problems to the office and talk about them on office time. These same people take the office problems home to their family and friends. The problem is you never get a rest from any of your problems, and you are not giving your best at either place. Both office and home problems are always there, and this causes stress, and stress causes disease and illness. You need to tune out your personal problems while you work, and tune out the office problems when you are home. This will lead for a much more relaxed life, much more energy to tackle these problems, and better health. You will be your best at work and your best at home.

Hard work is part of life. It can be destructive, or it can be a great sense of accomplishment to your soul; plus, it gives something back to this world.

Live Each Day as if It Were Your Last

The Essence of Today

> I expect to pass through this world but once. Any good I can do, or any kindness that I can show, let me do now, for I shall not pass this way again.

Essence of a New Day

> This is the beginning of a new day. You have been given this day to use as you will. You can waste it or use it for good. What you do today is important because you are exchanging a day of your life for it. When tomorrow comes, this day will be gone forever; in its place is something that you have left behind…let it be something good.

Only God knows the timing of our departure from this earthly plane. Today could be your last day here. Only people who have been told by doctors or the hangman know the number of days they have left. Stop a minute and ask yourself, *If this is really my last day here, how do I want to spend it?* Do you want to be angry over a comment someone made about you, or you didn't get the car of your dreams, or the little lady you had your eye on said no about going out, or your spouse or children are driving you crazy? Is this how you want to leave things here? Are these petty issues, or real problems that do need your attention? Don't waste your time on petty issues. That doesn't mean you don't have to deal with them because this might not be your last day, but have a different attitude about them. Don't let them become life or death issues. There is an expression that says, "don't sweat the small things." Things are small things. Relationships are big things. Put your energy into the big things and deal with the small things. If you do so, when you leave here, you can leave in peace.

Living this way will allow you to focus on the important stuff in life. It will free up your mind and energy to concentrate on the important things. You will find you spend less time on getting things and spend more time on building lasting relationships with others, especially your loved ones. Concentrating on getting things will cause you to miss why you are here. Remember, things are temporary, but the relationships we build and nourish will last for eternity. Concentrate on the eternal aspects of your life. I am not saying to ignore the things we need in this life to stay alive, but imagine standing before God, him asking what you did with your life, and you saying that you got a $400,000 house, a big Mercedes, and a big fat bank account. God will want to know what you did with your life, not what you bought. How did you treat others? Did you give to the poor? Did you help a neighbor or friend in need? Was your life a life of giving or a life of taking? If you concentrate on the giving, God will say, "Job well done, my son, come on in and rest."

When you realize what I am saying, you will be surprised at how liberating this can be. Not getting things can be disappointing, but they should never be sorrowful. It's okay to seek things, but never sell your soul for them. So many people stay in jobs they hate because of money. Just imagine forty years, five days a week, eight hours a day, doing something that is not fulfilling or beneficial to mankind. What a waste of a life.

When you live a life that cherishes each day it is a joyous life. Most of the normal BS most people focus on just seems to disappear when you appreciate each and every day. You will enjoy all of the good things that are here and not waste a single day on the things that are not really important. You will be able to look back over your life with pride.

As you get on with your life, ask other people what their dreams are, what they plan to do with their life, and most people will tell you things like, "I want to make enough money to buy a new car," or "I want to have a house on the beach," and so on. I believe these people are missing the most important things in life. Try to avoid spending too much time with these people. It is easy to be pulled into their narrow world. If someone says they want a house at the beach so they can spend more time with their family, teach their children about the ocean and nature, or they want a new car so they can take their children on a nice trip so the family can have some good quality time together—these are the people you should spend time with. They get it. Do you? Choose your friends and family carefully.

Learn to Relax

Priorities

A hundred years from now it will not matter what my bank account was, the sort of house I lived in, or the kind of car I drove...but the world may be different because I was important in the life of a child.

Attitude

Attitude is more important than the past, than education, than money, than circumstances, than what other people think or say or do. It is more important than appearances, giftedness or skill. It will make or break a company, a church, a home.

The remarkable thing is, we have a choice every day regarding the attitude we will embrace for that day. We cannot change our past. We cannot change the fact that people will act in a certain way. We cannot change the inevitable. The only thing we can do is play on the one string we have, and this is our attitude. (Charles Swindoll)

This topic may seem a little odd after all the other things I have said about studying hard, working hard, being of service to others. Growing up with my family, you know that I enjoy laughing, I enjoy life, and I have fun. It may not be clear to you, but I always do what I need to do first, and then I play. I don't play until and unless I have taken care of business first. I take my work seriously, I take my obligations of the house seriously, and then I take my play seriously too.

So how do you relax? This will change over time. Years ago, running ten to fifteen miles a day was relaxing to me. Right now at this stage of my life, that is not so. I enjoy just sitting on our new porch with a good CD playing, reading a book. That is very relaxing to me. It probably sounds like torture to you, so don't rely on what other people do—do what is relaxing for you. Over the years I have had many things that relaxed me. Building and remodeling our old house, playing soccer with my friends, hiking, and just being with my friends. All of these things had meaning to me. They gave me satisfaction, and they gave me a sense of peace. This is what relaxing is all about.

Take a walk or a jog after a long day of studying or working. This is very cathartic. It clears the mind, exercises the muscles, gets the blood moving, pushes toxins out of the body, and gives your brain a boost. It not only makes your body feel good, but it also gives you time to reflect on what you have done (studied), and it gives a sense of satisfaction. Relaxing is just as important as working, but remember, relaxing comes after you have done the work. Relaxing before you have worked is screwing off. This is not the path to success. It is the path to failure.

Laughter is also a good way to relax. Laughter is a tonic for the body and brain. If you can laugh during the tough times, you will come out of the troubles quicker, healthier, and better positioned to continue on your path. You have a great sense of humor, and I have seen you use it. Understand how you feel, understand how you have felt at troubled times in the past, understand how you have used your humor to overcome the problems and the emotions of those problems, and I know you will be able to carry this gift into the future.

I can't and won't tell you what you need to do to relax. It is a personal thing, and it is very different for each person. Find yours, and use it to balance your life. Don't use destructive things to help you relax. Too many people use drugs, alcohol, sex…as their relaxation. These things will ultimately lead to more problems, create more stress, and require more things to create relaxation. These people will be lucky to pull themselves out of this downward spiral. Some will go on their doom; some will realize where they are and pull themselves out. Be aware of where you are, and you will save yourself a ton of trouble in the future. Look to things that are positive—yoga, reading, walking, hobbies, karate, astronomy—the list is endless and exciting. Get an excitement about learning, and you will find that you will have many options that are fun, productive, and give you a great sense of calm.

Enjoy Life

Happiness

> Most folks are about as happy as they make up their minds to be. (Abraham Lincoln)

> Happiness doesn't depend on any external conditions, it is governed by our mental attitude. (Dale Carnegie)

This is a little different then living each day as if it were your last. The first implies your life is short (and it may be), and that you should concentrate on the important things in life. Enjoying life, on the other hand, implies that you should plan on a long life, filled with adventures, love and joy. Life is not a destination, it is not a dress rehearsal—it is a conscious act that can have wonderful consequences. Many people have what is called a midlife crisis. This is when people in their forties or fifties stand back, look at where they are in life, and realize this is not where they intended to be. It can create severe crises and often severe life changes, often very disruptive changes. If you enjoy life each day, you will be able to step back every so often, look at where you are, where you want to go, and not panic. So what if you are not there? You have enjoyed the journey to where you are now. If you need to change directions, just get about making the changes. Don't panic, don't have a crisis, just figure out what you need to do next, and enjoy the journey to the next level. The destination is important as I discussed in the goals section, but the journey is just as important. You need to constantly look back in addition to looking forward, but don't forget to enjoy both.

I saw a great little saying that goes like this, "Work like you don't have to, love like you have never been hurt, and dance like no one is watching." Great saying! All areas of your life will improve if you have this kind of attitude. Remember this, my son, you need to live your life—not the life others think you should live. Do the things you love to do (assuming they are legal, moral, and don't hurt others), love the people you want to love, live the kind of life you want to live, and be the person you want to be. Too many people try to live lives that others want them to live, and there is no happiness in that. They are so concerned about what others will think or say. Again, if it is legal, moral, and doesn't hurt another, do it!

After eighteen years of knowing me, you know that I live by this slogan. People often don't know what to make of me. This is not an act on my part. I have my own destiny, and I intend to live it. If someone has a problem with who I am, that is their problem. I don't fit into molds, I don't live my life by their rules—I trust my inner voice and I just go about living my life. It can be a little rough at times, but I know at my vaunted age of fifty-one, I can honestly say that I have lived *my* life—the good, the bad and the ugly—but it was and still is *my* life. I suggest you do the same.

Son, there is only one you. Be you, enjoy you, become the best you there is. Waking up thirty years from now and not recognizing yourself is such a waste. Be nice, be kind, be loving, be giving, but be you. If you don't like who you are, change. Improve you every day and enjoy the process. You will have regrets, you will wish you had done something different or better, but you will be so much better off in the long run if live your life for the reasons you were sent here. Listen to that small voice within; it is God talking to you. He created you, and he wants you to be you. He has a mission for you in this lifetime. It is your job to figure out what this mission is and to get about doing it. As they said in the *Shawshank Redemption* movie, "Get about living or get about dying."

Love

Love Is

If I speak with the tongues of men and of angels, but do not have love, I have become a noisy gong or a clanging cymbal.

And if I have the gift of prophecy, and know all mysteries and all knowledge; and if I have all faith, so as to remove mountains, but do not have love, I am nothing.

And if I give all my possessions to feed the poor, and if I deliver my body to be burned, but do not have love, it profits me nothing.

Love is patient, love is kind and is not jealous; love does not brag and is not arrogant, does not act unbecomingly;

It does not seek its own, is not provoked, does not take into account a wrong suffered, does not rejoice in unrighteousness, but rejoices with the truth; bears all things, believes all things, hopes all things, endures all things. love never fails...

When I was a child, I used to speak as a child, think as a child, reason as a child; when I became a man, I did away with childish things...

But now abide faith, hope, love, these three; but the greatest of these is love. (1 Corinthians 13)

I debated if this chapter should be first or last in this little book. I settled on last only because we often remember the last item we read or hear the best, and I believe this is the most important chapter of all. I don't know for a fact, but I would guess that love is the leading topic of most books written since the invention of the printing press. As Paul says in 1 Corinthians, you can have everything—knowledge, power, wealth—but unless you don't have love, you have nothing.

There are many kinds of love. The most encompassing is God's love for us. This is an unconditional love. A love so strong that not only did he create us, but He also gave us chance after chance to learn to do what is right. It is hard to explain this type of total love, but when you become a father, you will have a glimpse at what this feels like.

The next type of love is the love of a parent for their child. *The Prophet* by Kahlil Gibran has a passage on children that I think says it all. I would like to quote his thought on children from this book:

> Your children are not your children.
> They are the sons and daughters of Life's longing for itself.
> They come through you but not from you,
> And though they are with you yet they belong not to you.
> You may give them your love but not your thoughts,
> For they have their own thoughts.
> For their souls dwell in the house of tomorrow, which you cannot visit, not even in your dreams.
> You may strive to be like them, but seek not to make them like you.
> For life goes not backward nor tarries with yesterday.
> You are the bows from which your children as living arrows are sent forth.

The archer sees the mark upon the path of the infinite, and He bends you with His might that His arrows may go swift and far.

Let your bending in the archer's hand be for gladness;

For even as He loves the arrow that flies, so He loves also the bow that is stable.

This has been my quandary as your dad. How do I impart all that I have learned without making you a clone of me? I have always tried to encourage you to be you. There were times that I had to intervene as a dad and make you do certain things because it just had to be done. You are now in charge of you. As you get ready to leave for college, I am sending you out as a living arrow, for you to take your place in this world as an adult and for you to make your mark on this world. It is both with gladness and sadness that I send you, and most of all, it is with love.

There is, of course, the love of friends. I know as guys we don't like to use the word *love* unless there is a lady involved, but your closeness with your friends is a pretty strong and powerful emotion. I met three of my closest friends the first year of college, and thirty-three years later, I am still friends with these same people. The bonds you build in college will last a lifetime. Cherish your friends and make sure you are a good friend to them. Be there for each other, help each other, and keep each other safe.

Finally, there is the love of that special someone. The God love is something that just is. The love between parent and child is also just there. (Of course, there are examples of really bad kids and parents.) Friendships are strong, but the love between you and that special someone is different from the rest. This kind of love is a connection that touches the soul. There is a connection that can't be explained. It feels as if you just found the other half of yourself that you didn't even know was missing. Some people believe that we were created as twin souls, and that sometime in the past, we were divided. If that is true, you have a true soul mate out there. Many years ago, I asked how I would know when I was really in love. The answer was,

"You'll know." I have not been able to come up with a better answer for you. You will know. Something is just different. All of a sudden, nothing is important unless this person is involved. It is powerful and all-consuming.

So why can't we all find our soul mates and live happily ever after? Think about your own life. You have goals, dreams, and stuff to do. You may have already met your soul mate, and because you have so much going on in your head, you just didn't pick up the signals. This is why I mentioned the prayer and meditation earlier in this book. We need to slow down, get in touch with our inner self and our Creator, and "ask and it will be given."

Son, with divorce at 50 percent in our society, you could become a cynic very quickly. I hear both men and women saying how much they dislike the other sex, that they will never get married again, or they have just given up trying to find that special someone. Regardless of what happens to you, never give up. A failure on our part does not change the laws of the universe. Men and women are meant to be together. Families are the best way to bring up children. Yes, I know your mother and I got divorced a few years ago, and I am sorry for the grief it has caused you, but I am not soured on marriage and you shouldn't be either. It just didn't work out for us, so let's move on and start again.

Be careful you don't confuse lust with love. Physical looks are powerful for men. We are visual creatures. You could "fall in love" with a really beautiful woman just based on looks, but that will lead to disaster. It is interesting how the body reacts to love. There is a two-year period that the body produces endorphins when you fall in love. (This is the same happy juice the brain makes when you exercise.) This gives you those euphoric feelings you have when you are with that special someone. After two years, this stops, and unless you have some real bonds other than the physical, you will probably end up going your separate ways. For men, the physical is almost always the first thing that draws you to a woman, but you must work past that and really find out who this person is and if you share at least the big ideas of life. I believe the best marriages are ones that start as friends first and then blossom into love later.

As I have mentioned many times in this book, live your life, not other's. Choose the person who completes you. Choose someone with a good heart, good religious beliefs (these will give your life guidance and protect you in times of trouble), and someone who understands that being in a loving relationship does not mean giving 50/50 each. It must be 100 percent each, or it will not work. When one person wants more or, worse, expects more than they are willing to give, there will be trouble. Take your time, choose carefully, and then and only then, bring a child into this world. As in all things, ask your Maker what to do and then listen.

Epilogue

Well, my fingers are tired, and my head hurts from all this thinking and typing, so let's finish. I struggled for a number of years on which ten topics to pick. I am sure if I started this again, I would pick a few different ones, but regardless, I hope I have given you a few ideas to use with this new life of yours. I have also included a couple of additional sayings at the end of this book just because I liked them, and they didn't fit anywhere in the other chapters.

You already have everything you need to succeed inside of you. Having knowledge is not the same as using this knowledge. Regardless of our age, we are all children of God. We all have the same inheritance, we all have the same obligations, and we all must live by the same rules if we are to return to our Maker. I just happened to get to this earth thirty-three years before you and found some of this stuff before you did.

I am not my father. I am not my mother. I am a product of their upbringing, but I am uniquely me. This applies to you too. There is only one Duncan Erik Sylves. Take what you have learned from me, from your mom, from everyone else that had a hand in getting you to where you are today and use it for good. Enjoy your life, my son. I have observed you for eighteen years, and I am very confident you will do wonders. You have a great personality, you have good looks (I still say you got them from me, but whatever), you are funny, you have a great outlook on life, and you definitely have the brains. I have thoroughly enjoyed being your dad and spending the last eighteen years with you. Good luck with your college career and don't forget the "father quarters" on that big house you are going to build when you get that big job.

Dad

If

If you can keep your head when all about you are losing theirs and blaming
it on you;
If you can trust yourself when all men doubt you, but make allowances for their doubting too;
If you can wait and not be tired by waiting, or being lied about, don't deal
in lies,
Or being hated don't give way to hating, and yet don't look too good, nor
talk too wise;
If you can dream—and not make dreams your master; If you can think—and not make thoughts
your aim;
If you can meet with Triumph and Disaster and treat those two impostors
just the same;
If you can bear to hear the truth you've spoken twisted by knaves to make
a trap for fools,
Or watch the things you gave your life to, broken and stoop and build 'em
up with worn-out tools;
If you can make one heap of all your winnings and risk it on one turn of
pitch-and-toss,

And loose and start again at your beginnings and never breathe a
word
about your loss;
If you can force your heart and nerve and sinew to serve your turn
long
after they are gone,
And hold on when there is nothing in you except the Will which
says to
to them: "Hold on!"
If you can talk with crowds and keep your virtue, or walk with
Kings—
nor lose the common touch,
If neither foes nor loving friends can hurt you, If all men count with
you, but none too much;
If you can fill the unforgiving minute with sixty seconds worth of
distance run,
Yours is the Earth and everything that's in it, And—which is more—
you'll be a Man, my Son.

Rudyard Kipling

The Optimist Creed

P romise yourself—
To be so strong that nothing can disturb your peace of mind,
To talk health, happiness, and prosperity to ever person you meet.
To make all your friends feel that there is something in them.
To look at the sunny side of everything and make your optimism
come true.
To think only of the best, to work only for the best and expect
only the best.
To be just as enthusiastic about the success of others as you are about
your own
To forget the mistakes of the past and press on to the greater
achievements of the future.
To wear a cheerful countenance at all times and give every
living creature you meet a smile.
To give so much time to the improvement of yourself that you
have no time to criticize others.
To be too large for worry, to noble for anger, too strong for
fear and too happy to permit the presence of trouble.

(Note for Jr.: I was a member of the optimist club for many years,
and we stood and recited this creed at every weekly meeting. I think
is a good way to live your life.)

Serenity

G rant me the serenity to accept the things I cannot change
The courage to change the things I can
And the wisdom to hide the bodies of the people I had to kill because
they pushed me too far.

(Sorry, I had to get at least one joke in this.)

Duncan in grade school

Duncan at a graduation picnic

Duncan and me at my wedding Sep 23, 2017

About the Author

Craig has led a very active and varied life. Eagle Scout, Sunday school teacher, ordained deacon, college degree, soccer player, soccer coach, mountain hiker, extensive traveler throughout the US and Europe, long-distance runner (over 250 races), downhill skier, holder of six professional designations in insurance and risk management, partner in an insurance agency and two travel agencies, author of insurance articles for a local business publication, fifth-degree black belt, karate instructor for forty years teaching over two thousand students, guest lecturer at Penn State University regarding safety and risk management concepts, safety inspector all over the country, and an avid reader—especially biblical history.

With all that said, Craig says he has a good family, good neighbors, good friends, a nice house, a comfortable lifestyle, but the most important part of his life is being called Dad and now Grandpa. Life should be so good!

CPSIA information can be obtained
at www.ICGtesting.com
Printed in the USA
LVHW071508300822
727196LV00022B/1368